TOTEM POLES

OF THE

JAMESTOWN S'KLALLAM TRIBE

THE ART OF DALE FAULSTICH

Foreword by W. Ron Allen, Tribal Chairman
Carvings designed and executed by Dale Faulstich
S'Klallam Folk Tales reinterpreted by Dale Faulstich
Photographs by David Woodcock
Edited and with additional text by Joan Worley

Totem Poles of the Jamestown S'Klallam Tribe
Worley, J.

First Edition

Published by the Jamestown S'Klallam Tribe
1033 Old Blyn Highway
Sequim, Washington 98382
www.JamestownTribe.org

ISBN 978-0-9794510-0-3

Library of Congress Control Number: 2007928509

English text in this book is set in Calligraphic 421 BT.
Klallam words included in the text are set in Gentium,
a unicode format created by Victor Gaultney.

Design consultation, layout and typesetting:
Lobo Designs, Sequim, Washington
www.Lo-Bo.com

Print Executors:
Citicap Channels Ltd., New Delhi, India
www.citibazaar.com / connect@citibazaar.com

Cover Photos:
David Woodcock
www.GreywolfPhotography.com

TABLE OF CONTENTS

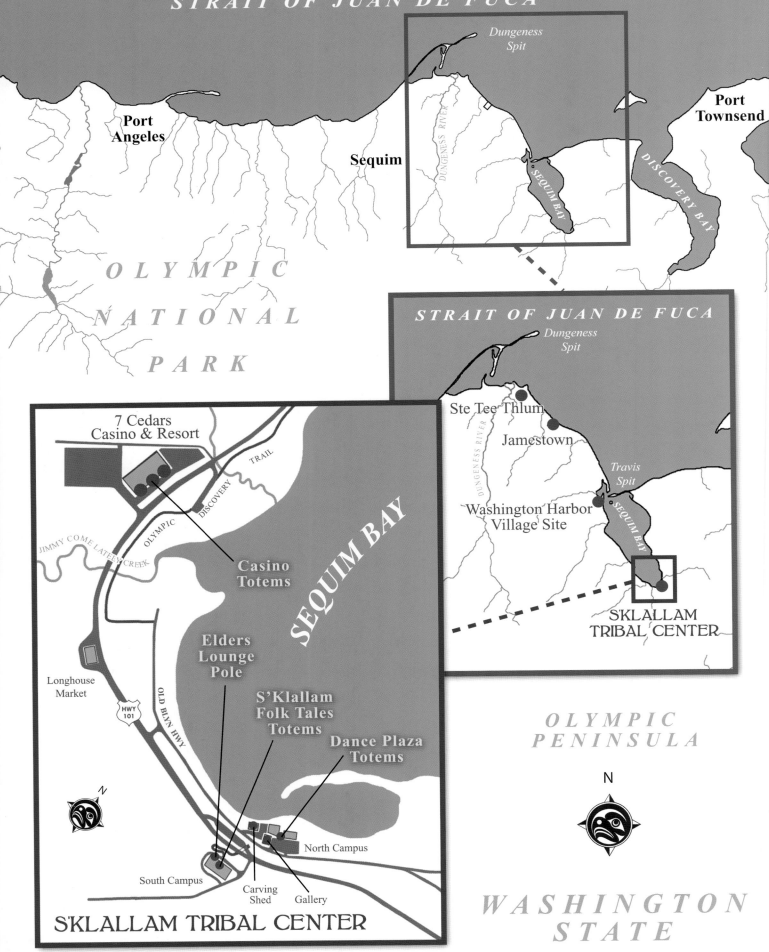

STRAIT OF JUAN DE FUCA

Dungeness Spit

Port Angeles

Port Townsend

DUNGENESS RIVER

SEQUIM BAY

DISCOVERY BAY

Sequim

O L Y M P I C

N A T I O N A L

P A R K

STRAIT OF JUAN DE FUCA

Dungeness Spit

Ste Tee Thlum

Jamestown

DUNGENESS RIVER

Travis Spit

Washington Harbor
Village Site

SEQUIM BAY

SKLALLAM
TRIBAL CENTER

O L Y M P I C

P E N I N S U L A

N

**7 Cedars
Casino & Resort**

TRAIL

DISCOVERY

OLYMPIC

JIMMY COME LATELY CREEK

**Casino
Totems**

SEQUIM BAY

**Longhouse
Market**

HWY
101

OLD BLYN HWY

**Elders
Lounge
Pole**

**S'Klallam
Folk Tales
Totems**

**Dance Plaza
Totems**

N

North Campus

South Campus

**Carving
Shed**

Gallery

SKLALLAM TRIBAL CENTER

N

W A S H I N G T O N

S T A T E

FOREWORD

Greetings,

On behalf of the Jamestown S'Klallam Tribal Council, I want to welcome and encourage you to use this book to better understand the purpose, value and cultural importance of the totem poles that grace our facilities and properties. Our Salish culture has a long history of using totem poles for many reasons, including commemorating family and community history, and the folklore of our religious, cultural and traditional beliefs.

In the Pacific Northwest, from the Washington/Oregon coast to the upper reaches of southeast Alaska, totems are prevalent in our villages for the reasons stated above, as well as to welcome our guests and visitors. We are very proud of our heritage and history, so we have chosen to commission our Master Carver and designer Dale Faulstich and carver/painter Nathan Gilles to transform old growth cedar trees into beautiful majestic totem poles. They have also spent many hours guiding our dedicated volunteer carvers in this traditional artistic expression of our cultural values.

The Jamestown S'Klallam Tribe is originally one of over twenty-two different S'Klallam villages that were spread out from the Hoko River region, in the western reaches of the Strait of Juan de Fuca, east to the Port Townsend area, and down the Hood Canal to the Hamma Hamma River region. Our village, north of Sequim inside of the Dungeness Spit, was one of the largest villages. As history changed our location, we eventually settled our Tribal operations, in the 1980's, to the Blyn area on Sequim Bay. Our Tribe has gradually been developing this Blyn site into our Tribal government and business campus. As we expand our operations and build new facilities or businesses, we have commissioned our carvers to design additional totems to remind our Tribal citizens of their history and heritage and to create a memorable experience for our visitors and guests.

We have been asked countless times to explain the meaning or story behind each totem, so our Master Carver Dale Faulstich has produced this book to explain the history of the poles and the story each pole symbolizes. We hope you enjoy the book's photos and narrative, and come to a deeper appreciation of each totem pole, as well as the incredible artistic talent of our carvers.

S'Klallam means "the Strong People." We are proud of our heritage and history. Our hope is that these poles will cause all who see them to have a deeper appreciation and respect for our people, culture, and contributions to our community. These Totems welcome now and for generations to come all visitors and guests to our territory, the gateway to our beautiful Olympic Peninsula.

Sincerely,

W. Ron Allen
Tribal Chairman/Executive Director

I

ACKNOWLEDGEMENTS

The art illustrated in this book could not exist without the encouragement and guidance of W. Ron Allen, chairman of the Jamestown S'Klallam Tribe; without the generous support of Tribal Councils, past and present; without the inspiration and advice provided by many citizens of the Jamestown S'Klallam Tribe. I feel especially honored to be entrusted with translating into three dimensions some of the heritage and culture of this Tribe. I have taken this trust to heart, and I have done my best to justify it.

Native art of the Northwest Coast cannot be separated from the culture that inspired it. For me, a journey of more than twenty years toward understanding both the culture and the art has left an indelible impression, giving me a deep respect for the sources of this artistic tradition. I stand in debt to the Native Northwest Coastal artists whose creations fill museum display cases the world over. I am also grateful to the storytellers, who have kept alive the tales - of past adventures, of fabulous creatures, and of the people who inhabit the Pacific Northwest Coast.

All of us involved with this book wish to convey special thanks to Elaine Grinnell, Jamestown Tribal Elder and storyteller, for sharing her stories and for graciously giving her permission to adapt three of them for this book; and to Kathy Duncan, Jamestown S'Klallam cultural historian, who served as an essential source and counsel in preparing the text.

Patsy Adams of the Jamestown S'Klallam Library provided expert support to our research for the book.

We also thank Ann Sargent, Jamestown S'Klallam Tribe executive assistant, who assumed countless administrative burdens to complete the publishing project.

Betty Oppenheimer, publications specialist for the Jamestown S'Klallam Tribe, helped with the details of copyrights, ISBN, Library of Congress codes, pricing and marketing.

This book owes its design to Laurie Tanguay of Lobo Designs, who also guided us through the printing process.

We found accurate versions of S'Klallam words and phrases on The Lower Elwha Tribe's website (www.elwha.org) and on the Klallam Wordlist site of Professor Timothy Montler, University of North Texas (www.ling.unt.edu/~montler/Klallam/WordList).

For the carving project, Peter Wagner of Pacific Western Timbers, Inc. was invaluable in acquiring the quality cedar logs used for the sculptures.

On a final, personal note, I wish to thank my wife Heather Faulstich for thirty years of companionship, support, and encouragement - and for her forbearance on those days when I came home tired, grumpy, and covered in wood chips.

Dale Faulstich

INTRODUCTION

STORIES TOLD IN WOOD

If it were not for the trees and hilly terrain, you could probably stand at one end of the Jamestown S'Klallam Tribe's property at Blyn and see all the totem poles, each standing tall, each painted in its distinctive Northwest style.

But you could not see the details, the intricate carving, and the patterns of color. To see all that, to read every story in wood, you must stand before each pole, close enough to see the images, to hear the wood speak.

The totem poles tell stories of many kinds, stories by and about the S'Klallam, known as "the Strong People."

Some stories originate in historical events, for example the peacemaking efforts of the S'Klallam leader T'Chits-a-ma-hun. During a tense period in 1857, he counseled other S'Klallam chiefs to spare the lives of white settlers despite stolen land and broken treaties. For ten days T'Chits-a-ma-hun argued his case. At the close of each day's council he signaled from Sentinel Rock to anxious white leaders that the S'Klallam had spared them - for one more day.

That is a story from history. A story derived from folklore is the tale of Coyote dancing almost to his doom in lusty pursuit of the Seashell Maidens.

And here is another - but who can say if this one is history or legend? Did Slap'u, the Wild Woman, ever roam these lands, looking for children to gobble up? Did old Ts'atsqwehe really save the children by luring Slap'u into Sequim Bay, where she drowned? You doubt it? Then what about the whirlpool - you can see it to this very day - that Slap'u made as she sank?

Other stories the poles tell were inspired by individual acts of honor, or of courage. Some recount adventurous exploits. Some, like that of the great leader T'Chits-a-ma-hun, derive from natural or political events. Others are more mysterious, inspired through ritual ordeals - acts of cleansing, fasting, journeys of isolation, as men and women sought the aid of a spirit guardian.

How did these stories reach the carvers of the totem poles? By many routes: through written history, as we have noted; through oral tradition, stories told over and over to many generations of the S'Klallam people - stories embedded in myth and fable, in Tribal memory.

No doubt some part of the stories as they are told here came to the carvers, as they slept, as they walked through these trees, along these paths. Every carver tells a story also, through a chip of cedar here, a touch of paint there.

This book tells one more story: of the people who planned and created the Jamestown S'Klallam Totem Poles.

THE JAMESTOWN S'KLALLAM TRIBE

S'Klallam Tribal history began many centuries ago on the Olympic Peninsula. The Jamestown S'Klallam Tribe's current property on Sequim Bay, however, was purchased only recently, after the Tribe achieved federal recognition in 1981. The Tribe chose this land - now the site of the Community Center, Administration Building, Dental Clinic, Library, Art Gallery, Casino, and Social Services Building - to provide a central location for citizens of the Tribe, most of whom live in Jefferson and Clallam counties.

Tribal Chairman W. Ron Allen puts it this way: "We see this place as a gateway to the Olympic Peninsula. The totem poles are a way to make a strong lasting impression on visitors to our home."

The first few poles were part of the Tribal Council's plan for the 7 Cedars Casino. Dale Faulstich, a non-native local artist already working with the Tribe on many projects, undertook exhaustive research on Northwest Art and studied with some of the Northwest's eminent carvers before making his first drawings for the Casino Poles. His care for the traditions and art of the S'Klallam earned him the position of lead carver, a reflection of the Tribe's confidence in his work.

The Tribal Council specifies the number and type of totem poles for each site. After the Council approves his designs, Faulstich and his team of carvers begin their work.

THE MEDIUM

Each totem pole pictured in this book was carved from a single specimen of Western Red Cedar, a tree 500 to 900 years old. These trees are harvested from the Hoh Rain Forest on the western side of the Olympic Peninsula.

The scientific name for this tree is <u>Thuja plicata</u>. Its S'Klallam name is xpáy. Throughout their history the S'Klallam have used Western Red Cedar in many ways. The huge trunks provided rot-resistant posts and lumber for longhouses. Canoes carved from single cedar logs served travelers, traders, fishers, whalers, and warriors.

Examining an old growth log for defects prior to the first cut.
Photo by Dennis Collins

No part of the Red Cedar was wasted. Thousands of years ago the S'Klallam learned to remove its heavy, stringy bark in strips without doing harm to the tree. Strips of inner bark could be woven into mats, room dividers, capes, skirts, rain gear, and hats. The Tribal people learned to pound the bark fiber into a cloth-like material soft enough to make sponges, towels - even diapers.

S'Klallam women, expert weavers, made cedar baskets used to collect and store food. Some they wove so fine as to be watertight. A S'Klallam cook could fill such a basket with water, put in meat or plants, then add hot stones to cook the food within. Bentwood cedar boxes were made to store necessities and ceremonial objects. The box might be secured with cord woven from cedar roots and withes (long, flexible limbs.) The S'Klallam also used cedar cord for fishing lines, nets, and snares for small animals.

The S'Klallam chose cedar wood for the shafts of spears and arrows. They pounded peeled roots to make paintbrushes. From the needles they brewed medicines to cure everything from headache to lung disease. Wounds were bound with bandages of softened bark.

It is no wonder that the S'Klallam stopped to honor Red Cedar before harvesting parts of the tree. Nor is it surprising that the S'Klallam became expert loggers, carpenters, weavers, canoe builders, and woodworkers. The artistry of early S'Klallam carvers can be seen in boxes, figurines, whorls (used to spin yarn from wool), carved fishhooks, combs, and a hundred other everyday items.

Although the S'Klallam could harvest bark, withes, and even planks from the standing tree, the process of felling a tree, to make a totem pole or a canoe, was both delicate and dangerous.

The loggers first chopped a shallow cut into the trunk with stone adzes. Into this hollow they kindled a small fire to char the wood. Laboriously alternating between adze and fire, they could cut through the huge trunk and, with care, control the tree's fall. As you might guess, most contemporary carvers forego this traditional method.

These adzes are based on original stone or shell tools used by early Native woodcarvers. Shown from left to right: "D" adze, straight adze, lip adze and finishing adze.

TYPES OF TOTEM POLES

Northwest Tribes use the term "totem pole" to denote a large spectrum of carved wooden columns. Forms and uses vary, depending on tribe, region, and circumstances. Here are some examples:

Freestanding pole: Raised in proud isolation, this elaborately carved pole displayed the hereditary crest figures belonging to the tribal leader who commissioned its creation.

Welcome figure: Usually a single human image on a pole, this carving greeted guests to a feast or potlatch.

Memorial pole: This freestanding pole presented crest figures and images associated with a deceased relative.

Mortuary pole: A special type of memorial to a dead leader, this totem pole also served as a repository for the great person's remains.

House Post: The S'Klallam frequently carved their totem figures on the large posts supporting the walls and roof of a longhouse. The carvings depicted guardian spirits and stories belonging to the extended family of the house.

Frontal pole: Set outside against the walls, house frontal poles also displayed the crests of the family who lived there.

DESIGNING AND CARVING THE POLES

You are welcome to visit the carving shed on the North Campus and watch the carvers as they work. Unless you plan a very long visit, however, you'll be able to see just a part of the process, for each totem pole is the result of at least 1500 hours of work.

Before the carving begins, Dale Faulstich submits to the Tribal Council his concept drawings, which show both front and side views of each totem pole. After the drawings are approved, Faulstich orders the logs for the poles. Since green wood is easier to work, especially in the tough end grain, Faulstich and the other carvers begin as soon as the logs arrive at the carving shed. The large adze is used first.

Though tools of ancient design, the adzes of today possess blades of steel instead of

Drawings by Dale Faulstich

stone or shell. Most versatile are the elbow adzes, V-shaped implements with handles formed from the natural elbow where branch meets trunk.

The lip adze, its four-inch-wide blade turned up at the ends, quickly removes bark and sapwood, two layers of the log that are not good carving wood. Once the carvers have prepared the log's surface, they square off the ends. A long notch is carved down the back of the log to relieve stresses that occur as the finished totem pole begins to dry.

Faulstich measures each log carefully. He adjusts his original concept designs to match the natural configuration of each log. Then he produces a meticulous scale drawing that will serve as a map for the carvers to follow.

To ensure the symmetry of the finished totem pole, the team snaps a chalk line down the log's center front. Following the latest scale drawings, Faulstich pencils in the first broad guidelines of the shapes to be carved. Here again, the lip adze will be used for the initial shaping.

Faulstich begins the modeling. He carves one side of each totem figure, anticipating and solving sculptural problems along the way. At each stage another skilled carver uses a large compass to transfer key points of Faulstich's work to the uncarved side of the log. Then he begins to match Faulstich's model as closely as possible.

Once the rough-out is complete, the carvers turn to more specialized tools. The slightly curved "clamshell" adze designed by Faulstich is used in the initial carving stages. A small straight adze, with no curve to its 2 1/2-inch blade, does finer work, and a D-shaped adze is wielded in tight places.

For detailed work of varying delicacy, the carvers employ a variety of chisels, gouges, and carving knives. Some are of European style, matching the tools the S'Klallam acquired by trade in the nineteenth century.

Other tools, although of steel, retain the original S'Klallam design. The graceful swoop of one carving knife (shown on page 8) mimics in steel the shape of the blade used before metal became available: the tooth of a beaver.

Drawings by Dale Faulstich

After the figures have been carved, the wood is given a traditional textured surface with a finishing adze. With its small (1 1/2-inch) blade and springy elbow handle of yew wood, the finishing adze "pops out" wood chips as the carver works, allowing for more control of the final texture.

Horizontal elements, like the wings of Thunderbird on the Elders Lounge Pole, are carved from heavy laminated slabs of cedar and attached during a later stage of the work.

The newly carved wood is beautiful in itself, but color establishes the traditional intensity of the totem poles. Two preservative coats of clear sealer are first applied. When these dry, base coats of a neutral color are used. The base color varies according to the color of the building to which the pole is assigned.

Then traditional colors - blacks, reds, and blue-greens - are added to dramatize the features of each figure on the pole. The carvers/painters study the brushwork for its effect on balance, composition, and harmony before creating the final sharp lines and striking contrasts that add power to the carvings.

THE CARVERS

<u>Dale Faulstich:</u> As a non-native working in a native tradition, Dale Faulstich enjoys a unique and long-standing collaboration with the Jamestown S'Klallam Tribe. Fascinated by the sophisticated art of the Northwest Coast's indigenous people, Faulstich researched and refined his art over twenty years to create original, contemporary objects with aboriginal themes. His art pays homage to the people who flourished on the Northwest Pacific Coast, to their culture, and to their long tradition of skilled woodworking. Faulstich also conducts carving classes for Tribal citizens (both youth and adult) and is a resource for other local carvers.

A number of skilled people have assisted Faulstich with these projects:

<u>James Bender:</u> Bender, a talented artist, was instrumental in the project's initial phase, working on the first three exterior poles at 7 Cedars Casino and two poles inside the Casino building.

<u>Loren White:</u> Five of the totem poles at 7 Cedars Casino owe much to White's hard work and amiable temperament.

<u>Steve Brown:</u> Three of the 7 Cedars Casino poles benefited from Brown's considerable knowledge and skill at carving.

<u>Nathan Gilles:</u> Since 2004, Nathan Gilles has established his ability as a carver and painter with his work on the Dance Plaza House Posts and the South Campus Poles. A valued collaborator in the ongoing project, Gilles is currently at work on poles for future sites.

<u>Ed Charles:</u> A citizen of the Lummi tribe with S'Klallam heritage, Ed Charles participated in carving the four Dance Plaza House Posts and the four South Campus Poles.

TOOLS ARE AN
EXTENSION OF BOTH
MIND AND HAND,
ENABLING THE
ARTIST TO TRANSFORM
INTENTION AND
AESTHETIC DESIRE INTO
PHYSICAL FORM

Dale Faulstich

<u>Bud Turner:</u> This painter's contributions can be seen on all the South Campus Poles.

<u>Harry Burlingame:</u> Retired Boeing engineer Harry Burlingame donated his time - and his twenty years of experience in Northwest style carving - to at least eight of the totem poles.

<u>Sam Barrell</u> and <u>Michael Donahue:</u> Both S'Klallam Tribal citizens, these young men are apprentice carvers who have worked on the project.

RAISING THE POLES

Mounting a completed totem pole - at once a 2000-pound log and a valuable piece of art - demands both power and finesse. Although traditionally a totem pole would have been raised by hand using a tripod of long poles, the contemporary process begins by leveling and preparing the installation site. Then specially manufactured steel supports are set upright into concrete.

The risky work of transporting and raising the huge poles requires heavy equipment and a light touch. Finished totem poles are padded and roped for protection, then hoisted by crane and loaded onto a flatbed truck for transport. At the designated site, the poles are again crane-hoisted and swung into position, the notched side of each against its matching steel support. Long bolts through pre-drilled holes join the totem pole to its support.

Photo by Joan Worley

DEDICATION CEREMONIES

Dedication of the totem pole is an occasion for warm greetings, celebration, and remembrance. The dedication may include prayer, dancing, singing, and recital of the pole's history and stories. Family members of a person honored on the pole may lead the way in the ceremony. Tribal members and guests are invited to bless the pole. In the tradition of the potlatch, gifts are presented and a meal is served.

COAST SALISH STYLE

The S'Klallam belong to the Coast Salish Tribes. While some of the Jamestown totem poles reflect carving done by other tribes in the region, most of the poles at Blyn are carved in Coast Salish style.

The Dance Plaza House Posts and the Strong People House Posts displayed on the next few pages were designed with the look of traditional S'Klallam house posts: the figures emerge from a background slab.

Step close to any of these poles and examine each figure's face to see characteristics typical of Coast Salish style. Each face, for example, is divided into three distinct planes.

The lip plane angles back steeply from the chin to the nose, and the mouth is a simple opening with little or no modeling of the lips.

The plane of the cheek is set deep below the plane of the forehead. The eye is carved directly into the cheek plane, with no eye socket or rounded eye orb. The shape of the eye is also severely constricted. The Wolf Mother (on the Legends Pole, page 16) has round eyes which narrow quickly to points just beyond their large, dark irises.

The nose extends from the forehead plane as a long, thin half cylinder shape with no nostril, or just a slightly shaped nostril.

Traditional paint colors of red, black, and blue-green are added to the poles in a somewhat geometrical style which does not follow the carved edges of the underlying face planes. The bands painted on the faces of Hal Ha Ske Nim (on the Founding Fathers Pole, page 14) and Ci'nakw (on the Legends Pole, page 19) show this characteristic.

Artists from the tribes of the Northwest Coast influenced each other, of course, as the totem poles at 7 Cedars Casino acknowledge. The carved designs on the 7 Cedars Poles incorporate many attributes of Northwest Coast Tribal art. Four of the poles at the Casino specifically honor the carving style of regional tribes shown on this map: the Kwakwaka'wakw, the Nuxalk, the Haida, and the Tlingit.

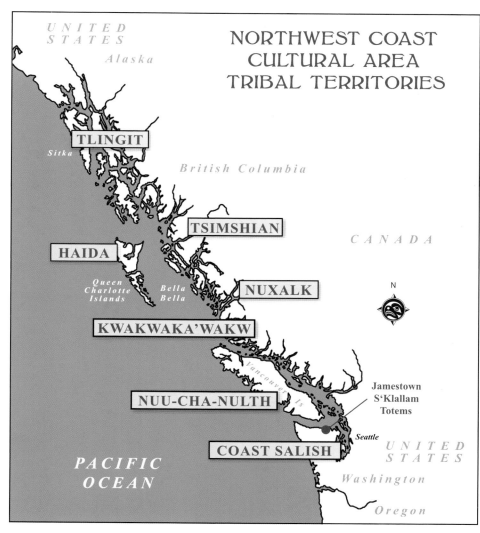

NORTHWEST COAST
CULTURAL AREA
TRIBAL TERRITORIES

UNITED STATES
Alaska

TLINGIT
Sitka

British Columbia

TSIMSHIAN

CANADA

HAIDA
Queen Charlotte Islands
Bella Bella

NUXALK

KWAKWAKA'WAKW

N

NUU-CHA-NULTH

Vancouver Is.

Jamestown S'Klallam Totems

Seattle

COAST SALISH

UNITED STATES

PACIFIC OCEAN

Washington

Oregon

THE DANCE PLAZA
HOUSE POSTS

Long ago, the S'Klallam built summer and winter village homes along the Olympic Peninsula of Washington. Although they were known among other tribes as "the Strong People," they faced a grave challenge after 1855. In that year, a hasty agreement with the U.S. government, the Point-No-Point Treaty, exchanged S'Klallam lands for a place on a crowded reservation one hundred miles away. Knowing their rights were not respected, many S'Klallam rejected the move.

In 1874 a group of S'Klallam families from several villages put their money together and bought legal title to 210 acres of the Dungeness River Valley at a place they named Jamestown in honor of Lord James Balch.

The Dance Plaza House Posts commemorate that united action, which ensured the Tribe a permanent place on traditional lands.

You will find these Dance Plaza House Posts in the parking lot in front of the Administration Building. (See the map at the front of this book.) The left-hand pole is dedicated to the Founding Fathers of the Jamestown S'Klallam Tribe. The right-hand pole presents legends and history unique to the Tribe.

THE FOUNDING FATHERS

STE TEE THLUM

Ste Tee Thlum, who lived in the mid-1700's, is represented by the bottom figure of the left-hand pole. He was hereditary chief of the village located where the Dungeness River flows into the Strait of Juan de Fuca. He married a princess from Nanaimo, a village on Vancouver Island in British Columbia. Many Jamestown Tribal citizens are directly descended from the large family of Ste Tee Thlum and his bride. Ste Tee Thlum's image on this pole holds eight feathers, representing his daughter and his seven sons.

HAL HA SKE NIM

Hal Ha Ske Nim, the figure carved just above Ste Tee Thlum, holds an image of the sun in his hands. In the late 1800's, Hal Ha Ske Nim was head chief of Suxtcikwi'in (sčqʷéʔyəŋ), or "quiet waters," the village located at the entrance to Sequim Bay. The bay itself and the town of Sequim take their names from the anglicized pronunciation of the S'Klallam word.

Hal Ha Ske Nim's village comprised ten longhouses, each the dwelling of an extended family. The largest of these houses, the potlatch house, belonged to Hal Ha Ske Nim. Inside his longhouse, carved on the log post that supported the roof beams, was an image of the sun - "The Shining One" - Hal Ha Ske Nim's guardian spirit.

T'CHITS–A–MA–HUN

T'Chits-a-ma-hun, grandson of Ste Tee Thlum, is the next figure on the pole. T'Chits-a-ma-hun lived from 1808 to 1888 and was known as a peacemaker and friend to early settlers. As a young man, he traveled by steamship to San Francisco. A sharp-eyed observer, he returned with new impressions of the power behind the white settlers then entering S'Klallam lands. Respect for their strength led T'Chits-a-ma-hun to befriend the settlers and to advise peace and trade to those of the S'Klallam who would make war on them.

During the "Indian Wars" of the 1850's, a gathering of tribal leaders proposed to drive the settlers entirely out of the region. For ten days in 1857, the S'Klallam debated whether to kill the settlers or spare their lives.

T'Chits-a-ma-hun argued for peace. After each day's council, he went to Sentinel Rock and signaled to the settlers with his blanket the course of the tribal leaders' debate. On the tenth day, he stood up, threw off his blanket, and shouted. The danger had passed, and the threat of war was over.

The settlers found T'Chits-a-ma-hun's name difficult to pronounce and called him "Chetzemoka." By any name, however, they were grateful to him, and eventually they installed a bronze plaque on Sentinel Rock to commemorate T'Chits-a-ma-hun's ten days of signals. In 1905, a park in Port Townsend, Washington was named in his honor.

LORD JAMES BALCH

Lord James Balch is the top figure of this totem pole. He is represented holding an Eagle and a Salmon, which are the crest figures of the Jamestown S'Klallam Tribe. In 1874, he organized the purchase of land near the traditional village site of Nuxia'antc, "the Village of the White Firs," not far from the village of Ste Tee Thlum. Under Lord James Balch's guidance, the S'Klallam purchased 210 acres for $500.00, and the land was divided into plots proportionate in size to each person's contribution. The new community of Jamestown, and later the Tribe itself, were named in his honor.

LEGENDS AND HISTORY

The intricate connection between the natural world, the spirit world and the human world shapes many S'Klallam legends. Figures on the right-hand house post in the Dance Plaza emphasize this bond in the history of the Tribe.

THE WOLF MOTHER

Before the area around Sequim Bay was heavily settled in the late 1800's, the region was full of wolves. The S'Klallam people could often hear them howling in the evenings. One legend even says the village of Suxtcikwi'in was founded by a family of wolves.

Long ago, the old story says, a lonely young princess fell in love with a handsome stranger who only came to meet with her at night. After a time, her mysterious lover disappeared, but the princess discovered she was pregnant. She gave birth to five wolf cubs, and for this shame her village cast her out.

Poor and abandoned, the young mother had no way to provide for her family except to dig shellfish. Each day she left her wolf children at home and went to the beach to dig. As she worked beside a small fire on the beach, she could often hear loud noises coming from her house, sounds as of people singing, dancing, and drumming. Yet only her wolf children were at home.

Determined to find out what was going on, the young mother set a trap. She went to the beach as usual one day, built her little fire, as usual, but on this day she stuck her digging stick into the sand and placed her cloak over it. Next to this she placed her basket, so from a distance it would look very much like she was there, hunched over, digging clams. Then she circled back through the woods and quietly approached the house. She peeked in.

There were her five wolf children, but what a change! They had removed their wolf skins and were actually human children, dancing, singing, and drumming away. Angry as any mother would be at this deceit, she burst into the house and scolded her misbehaving children.

16

The children felt guilty for being such a burden to their mother, and they vowed from that point on to help her in all things. The first son declared that he would become a hunter of sea mammals. The next said he would go to the forest and hunt for bear, elk, and deer. The third decided to become a fisherman and bring home salmon and halibut. The fourth son declared he would become a carver, carpenter, and canoe builder. The fifth wolf child, the daughter, promised to learn to weave blankets and baskets, to gather berries and roots for food.

These things they all did, developing the skills needed for the young family to survive, even to prosper. With the passage of time, this hard-working household developed into the village of Suxtcikwi'in, the name that, transformed, was given to the city of Sequim.

On the totem pole, the Wolf Mother is the bottom figure. She holds her digging stick and stands on designs meant to represent the beach where she dug shellfish for a living. Her skirt shows a decoration of wolflike patterns.

[Adapted by Dale Faulstich from "Dog Husband," told by David Prince in Klallam Folk Tales by Erna Gunther.]

THE WOLF CHILDREN

Above the Wolf Mother the human faces of the Wolf Children look out from the totem pole. At the sides of the pole, abstract wolf designs recall their animal nature.

C'I-NAKW
(čínəkʷaʔ)

C'i-nakw (čínəkʷaʔ), "thunder power" or "chain lightning power," was a special war spirit power that only the Dungeness S'Klallam possessed. A person with such a guardian spirit could call on this power to weaken his enemies and make them unable to defend themselves.

The power of C'i-nakw created an impressive ceremonial display as well. When the S'Klallam were invited to another village for a potlatch celebration, they approached the beach with their canoes lined up, one behind the other, in a zig-zag pattern imitating the course of lightning. The canoes would then line up abreast of each other, facing the beach. In the bow of each canoe stood a dancer arrayed in C'i-nakw regalia, singing the power songs of the S'Klallam.

Finally, the canoes would come into the beach together. The paddlers disembarked, then danced in a zig-zag line, single-file, to the longhouse. Inside, the dancers made four counterclockwise circuits of the central fire, still singing their power song.

Standing above the wolf children on the totem pole, the figure representing C'i-nakw wears the traditional dancer's regalia: a cedar bark headdress with seven feathers, an eagle tail fan in each hand, and a black design painted on his face.

[Based on information from Frank Allen and Henry Allen in Twana Narratives: Native Historical Accounts of a Coast Salish Culture by William Elmendorf.]

HAL HA SKE NIM'S HOUSE POST FIGURE

On the interior house posts of Hal Ha Ske Nim's longhouse were carved images of the sun - representing "The Shining One," the chief's guardian spirit. On posts outside the longhouse Hal Ha Ske Nim was directed by his guardian spirit to carve figures of birds with outstretched wings. The figure atop the Legends pole refers to this bond between the leader and his spirit guardian.

THE STRONG PEOPLE

Installed back-to-back with the Founding Fathers and Legends House Posts are two posts which face Sequim Bay and overlook the Dance Plaza itself. These are the Strong People House Posts. The crossbeam between them recalls an old story from the time when the coast tribes built their longhouses with massive cedar logs for support:

> The tribes of the area gathered once, faced with the task of lifting a particularly heavy house post. One by one, groups from each tribe tried to heft the huge log. One by one, they failed.

> The S'Klallam people considered the problem. They rolled the long pole into the water of Sequim Bay. As the log began to float, their strongest men stooped in the water to put their shoulders underneath. Then they stood, and by their combined strength they lifted the pole from the water and carried it to its place. From that day, the S'Klallam have been known as "the Strong People."

[Adapted from the story told by Elaine Grinnell in <u>The Jamestown S'Klallam Story</u> by Joseph H. Stauss.]

The two human figures, the strong men, support the crossbeam, which is carved with images of Wolf, an important guardian spirit of the tribe. The designs on the poles above the horizontal beam are based on designs from S'Klallam war clubs collected in 1792.

THE SOUTH CAMPUS POLES

S'KLALLAM FOLK TALES

Near the Social Services Building on the South Campus stands a cluster of three large totem poles, with a smaller pole outside the Elders' Lounge. Like the Dance Plaza House Posts, these four poles are carved in Coast Salish style.

When Dale Faulstich undertook the project, he spent many hours researching S'Klallam folk tales. Selecting the stories he wanted to reinterpret in wood was difficult; selecting the images to represent them was yet another challenge.

Mulling over the problem on his usual early walk one morning, Faulstich looked up to find a black bear regarding him curiously from the woods. Faulstich felt the encounter must mean something, so as the bear disappeared among the trees, he told it, "All right. I'll put you on the totem pole."

The next morning's walk was interrupted by the appearance of a coyote. "O.K.," the carver told the interested coyote, "You're on the totem pole, too."

A day later he found himself under the scrutiny of a deer. And the day after that a Douglas squirrel scampered up close to scold him for a good while before whisking away. Faulstich couldn't help promising the deer and squirrel their own places in the carving.

These early morning encounters helped determine which stories were selected for the project. Now, human visitors to the South Campus can see on the largest of the poles the influence of the artist's animal consultants.

The tallest pole, at forty-five feet, tells four stories: "The Battle with Northwind"; "Grizzly Bear and the Man-in-the-Moon"; "Coyote and his Helpers"; and "First Deer and First Kingfisher."

The twenty-two-foot pole represents three stories: "Slap'u"; "Beaver and the Great Flood"; and "The Boy who Disobeyed his Mother."

Two stories comprise the eighteen-foot pole: "A Warrior Receives the First Weapons" and "A Woman Marries a Killer Whale."

The Elders' Lounge Pole, twelve feet tall, presents the important Tribal guardian spirits Wolf and Thunderbird.

THE 45-FOOT POLE

THE BATTLE WITH NORTHWIND

Long ago, before the world came to be as it is today, the Northwind blew all the time, trapping the world in bitter cold. The people could not launch canoes to fish because white caps thrashed around Sequim Bay. They could not collect roots and berries because the plants were all frozen as solid as the ground.

Desperate, the people called a council and declared war on the Northwind.

The shivering, tattered army marched toward the enemy's house. Grizzly Bear (kʷəyéʔčən) said, "I am strong. I will wrestle Northwind to the ground."

Halibut (scúʔtx) was not to be outdone. "I have only to turn sideways," bragged the flatfish, "and his fury will blow past me."

Each of the animals boasted a special strength for the coming battle, except for little Squirrel and tiny Wren.

"No wonder they are so quiet," scoffed the others, "for they are the smallest and weakest of us all."

At the house of Northwind, the army of creatures bravely faced the worst of the cold. Grizzly Bear charged into battle. Northwind huffed even stronger and blew Grizzly away like a ball of fur. Halibut stepped in next, but Northwind's blast caught him like the sail on a boat, tossing him far off. Elk, Seagull, Deer, and the others were defeated in their turn. Only Squirrel (c̓aʔc̓psiʔúcən) and Wren (t̓aʔt̓əmʼ) were left.

Squirrel scampered up the backside of a large tree, out of the wind's force, and began to scold. He screeched. He chirped. He hollered. The noise enraged Northwind. No matter how hard Northwind blew, Squirrel kept up his chatter-chatter-chatter.

While Squirrel's insults distracted Northwind, Wren kept low, hopping along the ground from one small dip to another, keeping out of the wind's way, until he crouched behind Northwind. Wren took a breath, called upon his spirit power, and leaped up boldly, singing "I'm Wren! I'm Wren!" at Northwind's back.

Worn down by Squirrel's scolding and startled by Wren's song, Northwind tired, so that at last the two little warriors were able to tie him to a post in his own house.

"How long do you intend to blow?" Wren asked, when they had bound him fast.

"One hundred days," said Northwind.

"If you cannot behave better," declared Squirrel, "we will have to kill you." With the great wind in their power, Squirrel and Wren threatened and negotiated until Northwind agreed never to blow for more than four days in a row. The tiny warriors set Northwind free then, and to this day Northwind has never broken his promise.

[Adapted by Dale Faulstich from "The War with Northwind," told by Joe Johnson and Mrs. Johnson, translated by Johnson Williams, in Klallam Folk Tales by Erna Gunther.]

Designed by Dale Faulstich, this bronze disk represents Eagle and Salmon, the tribe's crest figures. This design may be found embedded in the Dance Plaza and on each end of the pedestrian underpass leading to the South Campus Poles.

GRIZZLY BEAR AND THE MAN-IN-THE-MOON

A long time ago, in a village on Dungeness Bay, the head chief and his wife had four sons but only one daughter. The mother warned her daughter again and again, "Never go into the forest alone."

One day, young women from the village went out to pick berries; the princess wandered off and got lost. While she was resting on a log by the river, deciding how to solve her problem, a handsome young man approached her. He was chewing some spruce gum, and she wished she could have some, too.

"Come," he said. "I'll show you to the tree where I found the gum."

The princess followed him deeper into the forest. They never came to the spruce gum tree, for the young man was actually Qweetc'en (kʷəyéʔčən), Grizzly Bear, in human form. He led the princess to his house and forced her to become his wife.

At the village on Dungeness Bay, the chief's wife sent her oldest son to look for his sister. He found her tracks by the river and beside them the tracks of a large bear. The brave young man followed the tracks and discovered his sister at the home of Grizzly Bear.

"You must leave right away!" the miserable princess told her

brother. "My husband is a very bad man. Leave, or you may die!"

At last she managed to talk her brother into going back. He had just left when Qweetc'en the bear came home and sniffed the air.

"There has been a person here. I can smell him," he told his wife. "I had better follow him and take him some food."

Grizzly Bear tracked his wife's brother and called to him: "Brother-in-Law! Wait! You should take this food with you."

When the brother turned to face him, Qweetc'en the bear slashed with his sharp claws and ripped out the man's heart. Grizzly Bear swallowed the heart right there and took the body back to store on a high shelf in his house.

One by one, the grieving mother sent her sons to rescue the princess. One by one they found her, but one by one Qweetc'en killed them all and threw their bodies onto the shelf.

When none of her children returned, the mother wept day and night. She pleaded with the Full Moon for help, and Full Moon took pity on her. As the mother cried day after day, she had saved all the mucus she cleared from her nose and hid it in the bark of a cedar tree. Now the mucus transformed into a child, and the child into a powerful young warrior who set out to rescue the princess.

Before he left the village, the young warrior took off his shirt and tied a flat rock to his chest, another to his back. He put his shirt on over this armor, picked up his weapons, and went deep into the forest to Qweetc'en's house.

"You had better leave," the princess warned this stranger. "My husband is very bad. See, he has killed all my brothers and stacked their bodies on that shelf."

The young warrior did not leave. He hid behind a house post instead. Grizzly Bear returned and sniffed the air.

"I smell a person," he said. "Come out of your hiding place."

The young warrior leaped out from behind the house post, and Qweetc'en the bear attacked, aiming for his heart. But all of Grizzly Bear's claws broke on the flat stones the warrior wore under his shirt. With Qweetc'en's claws went his strength, and the warrior was able to kill him with bow and arrows.

Then he opened up Grizzly Bear with a knife and pulled out the hearts of all the brothers. Placing each heart with its body, he returned each brother to life.

The young warrior took the princess and all her brothers home. The family was reunited, and the mother was overjoyed to have her children around her once more.

The young warrior, however, had accomplished his great task and now began to feel homesick. One night he looked to the sky and said to the Moon, "Father, it is time for me to come home."

To this day, you can look at the night sky when the moon is full and see Mucus Boy - or, as we call him, the Man-in-the-Moon - as he watches over us.

[Adapted by Dale Faulstich from "Mucus Boy," told by Boston Charlie, interpreted by Vera Ulmer, in Klallam Folk Tales by Erna Gunther.]

COYOTE AND HIS HELPERS

Coyote prowled the shore of Sequim Bay one spring morning, as usual up to no good. He heard beautiful singing.

Soon he came upon three lovely young women laughing and dancing on the beach. Instantly pricked by lust, Coyote watched them for a time, but when he approached they ran from him and jumped into the bay. Embarrassed, Coyote gave up - for that day.

The next day Coyote was back, and there they were - three young maidens singing, dancing, and laughing. Coyote's desire grew stronger. Again he drew near them, and again they ran off to dive into the water. Coyote persisted, but after four frustrating days, he grew angry. He turned for help to his two supernatural helpers, his constant companions - in short, his own scat.

"Little Brothers," he asked, "how can I get close to these women?"

After some discussion, his helpers gave their advice.

"Coyote," they said, "you should sing the same song as the beautiful maidens, and dance the same dance. Begin singing and dancing a long way down the beach and move very slowly toward them as you dance. Perhaps this way

Photo by Michael Francis

the maidens will not feel so threatened by your approach."

It was just the kind of trick Coyote liked, but he was too proud to take advice well.

"Of course!" he snapped. "That is exactly what I had already planned to do!"

The next day Coyote tried his luck once more on the beach. When he could hear the first notes of the maidens' song, he began to sing and dance. Very slowly he danced down the beach toward the women. Closer and closer.

By the time he was among them, he was infatuated, out of his head with love, and greedy for the pleasure to come.

But these maidens were no ordinary dancers. They were Seashell People, their home the bottom of Sequim Bay, and they changed into young women whenever they came out of the water to sing and dance.

They knew Coyote for a rogue and a trickster but pretended to be taken in by his ploy. One of them held his right arm as they all danced, another his left. The third danced behind him, rubbing his shoulders. This felt so good to Coyote that he didn't realize they were now dancing with their feet in the water. The maidens kept singing to him and laughing with him and dancing around him, all the while leading him deeper into the bay.

Caressing his arms and back, they sang, "We want to marry you, Coyote. We want to take you home with us and begin our honeymoon as soon as possible!"

Smitten, Coyote didn't even know where he was until the water was up around his neck. He began to squirm and thrash around. Too late!

The Seashell Maidens pulled him with them down to the bottom of the bay. They held him there until he drowned.

Poor Coyote. For four days he floated face down in Sequim Bay. At last he washed up onto the same beach where he'd first seen the maidens. His friend Wolf, out for a morning stroll, found Coyote lying in the sand.

As wise as Coyote was foolish, Wolf said, "Well, here's old Coyote. He must have tried fooling around with those Seashell People."

Wolf was a shaman, and he decided to help his friend. He searched the forest for medicinal plants, chewing on them as he walked back to Coyote on the beach. He spit the wad of plants he'd been chewing right onto Coyote's body and then recited some prayers. He stepped across the body of his friend four times. The last time he did so, Coyote woke up.

Coyote didn't know where he was or what had happened. Then he realized he was once more alive and growled, "Wolf, why are you bothering me while I'm asleep? I was having a nice little nap. Leave me alone!" He straightened up as well as he could, wrapped his dignity around him, and stumbled off down the beach.

Wolf watched Coyote walk away, and he laughed.

[Adapted by Dale Faulstich from the story told by Alice Williams, translated by Vi Hilbert in
Haboo: Native American Stories from Puget Sound.]

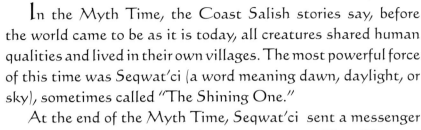

FIRST DEER AND FIRST KINGFISHER

In the Myth Time, the Coast Salish stories say, before the world came to be as it is today, all creatures shared human qualities and lived in their own villages. The most powerful force of this time was Seqwat'ci (a word meaning dawn, daylight, or sky), sometimes called "The Shining One."

At the end of the Myth Time, Seqwat'ci sent a messenger to rearrange the world into the way it is now. This Changer, or Transformer, traveled the world reshaping myth-age beings into the animals, places, and people we know today.

Coming from the East and moving toward the West, the Changer, called Nokui'metl by the S'Klallam, brought light with him as he traveled. Before his arrival all was dark; darkness fell again behind him; but it was light where he was.

The people knew that Nokui'metl was coming, and some did not welcome the changes he would bring. One man decided he would kill this Changer, so he went home and began to sharpen his knives, which were large mussel-shells filed into shape. As he worked, a stranger came to his house and asked what he was doing.

"I am going to kill this Changer who is coming," the man explained.

"Hmmm," said the stranger. "Why not put those shells on top of your head?"

The man found himself doing just that.

"Now, jump!" cried the stranger.

The man jumped. As he did, he was transformed into the first Deer (húʔpt), and those mussel shells were his ears.

Nokui'metl, for that's who the stranger was, traveled on. Soon he came to another house where he saw a woman sitting by the fire, stringing beads.

"What are you going to do with those beads?" he asked her.

Without a word, the woman put the strings of beads around her neck. As she did that Nokui'metl said, "Go! Fly, now!"

The woman changed into the first Kingfisher (čačšə́yə), and away she flew.

[Adapted by Dale Faulstich from the story told by Mrs. Robbie Davis in Klallam Folk Tales by Erna Gunther.]

30

THE 22-FOOT POLE

SLAP'U

All the tribes of the Central Coast Salish territory tell tales of the "Wild Woman of the Woods" or the "Basket Ogress." Huge and very hairy, she was only part human. The rest of her was an eerie supernatural being.

Under her heavy brow her eyes were sleepy, but when she pursed her lips and wailed "OOOOOOooooooooooooohhhhh!" she was the most fearsome thing in the woods.

In the Jamestown S'Klallam villages, people called her "Slap'u," and parents warned their children that if they wandered off from the village, Slap'u might capture them, stuff them into her large basket, and spirit them away to her home deep in the forest.

One day, not so very long ago, a young S'Klallam boy who lived in the village at Sequim Bay felt hungry. To tell the truth, this boy was always hungry, and in spite of his parents' warning he ventured out into the forest to find something more to eat.

He walked and walked, further and further from his village, growing hungrier and hungrier, more and more lost. Then, through the trees, he thought he heard a woman's voice. The voice offered him his favorite food - smoked salmon!

The boy could only see dark forest all around him, but the idea of a slab of smoked salmon made his mouth water, and he followed the voice still deeper into the woods.

There! On that log! A nice piece of smoked salmon! The boy ran forward to the salmon and took a bite. Pah! It wasn't salmon at all, just a piece of fir bark.

Before he could run away, however, Slap'u grabbed him and put him into the huge basket she carried on her back. Then she bounded toward her home in the center of the forest.

The miserable young boy bounced along in the basket, wishing he had listened to his parents. The thought of his family brought to mind a gift his father had just made him of a small mussel-shell knife. The boy brought out the knife and set to work cutting at the bottom of the basket.

Finally he cut a hole large enough; and carefully, so Slap'u wouldn't notice, he squirmed out through the hole. The instant his feet touched solid ground again, he began to run.

Still dreaming of the tasty meal the boy would make, Slap'u would have plodded along all day except that she stopped to rest. She swung the basket from her back and licking her lips, took a peek at her prize. But when she lifted the lid, all she saw was a big hole and the ground beneath. Slap'u's blood-curdling scream shook the forest, and she began to bound back the way she had come.

The boy heard the scream and ran swiftly as he could, desperate to find his way back to the village. He struggled through dense forest undergrowth, terrified, for he could hear Slap'u crashing through the trees behind him. Every few minutes her enraged shrieks made him jump. Exhausted, he was about to give up when the trees cleared, and he found himself on the shore of Sequim Bay.

But he was on the wrong side! He stood trembling on the eastern side of the bay, but his village was way over on the western shore. He knew there was no way across, just a small peninsula of land that ran partway across the mouth of the bay. The boy set out running along this spit of land, in the forlorn hope that someone would be out in the bay fishing. As he puffed to the end of the spit, with Slap'u thudding behind him, the boy saw Ts'atsqwehe, a village elder, out fishing for crab.

The boy called out to the fisherman, and the old man recognized him as the missing child. He pulled his canoe in to shore and took the boy aboard. As they paddled toward the village, the boy told Ts'atsqwehe how he'd been kidnapped and how Slap'u was chasing him.

The old fisherman returned the boy to his frantic parents, but he himself paddled back out to the mouth of Sequim Bay. Slap'u came clumping along the beach of the peninsula, tracking the boy by his footprints in the sand, and demanded that the old man take her across the channel.

Unafraid, Ts'atsqwehe paddled up and allowed the huge creature into his canoe.

"Stay in the bow of the canoe, though," he told her. "There are crabs in the bottom of the canoe and they're particularly angry about being caught today." Then Ts'atsqwehe, as he paddled, began to sing his spirit song. It was a fisherman's song to the crabs, asking them for help in this crisis.

The crabs responded. As Ts'atsqwehe sang, they crawled toward Slap'u in the bow. Slap'u saw them approaching her and screamed at the old man to call them back.

"Don't worry," he replied. "That's just the way crabs act. Back away from them."

Slap'u did this, but the crabs kept scuttling toward her, and when they got close they pinched her and bit her toes.

Of course Slap'u backed away more quickly, and when she did she toppled overboard. The old fisherman pretended to come to her rescue, but he actually poked her further underwater with his paddle. Slap'u was large and powerful, but she was also clumsy. And she couldn't swim. She sank rapidly to the bottom of the channel.

Even today, if you go to the mouth of Sequim Bay, not far from the end of Travis Spit, you'll see a whirlpool there, with air bubbles popping to the surface. This is the place where Slap'u sank.

[Adapted by Dale Faulstich from the story told by Elaine Grinnell in The Jamestown S'Klallam Story by Joseph H. Stauss.]

BEAVER AND THE GREAT FLOOD

The world was still very young, long ago, when the rain stopped falling and the earth became drier than it had ever been. Plants and trees withered and died, so there were no roots or berries to eat. Lakes and streams grew so shallow that the salmon and other fish could no longer live in them. The people were very hungry and very thirsty.

At this time, Beaver (ɬq̓táw̓əč) was a powerful shaman, respected and feared by all. The people came to Beaver and said, "The land is drying up. Send us water or we will die of hunger and thirst."

"Go home," Beaver told them. "Build sturdy canoes, strong enough to withstand a great storm."

Some of the people went home and started building large canoes. They stored up what little food and water they could. They twisted cedar bark into long ropes, as Beaver had also instructed them.

Other people did not bother to build canoes. "If a storm comes," they said, "we will simply walk to high ground."

Beaver went to a sacred place in the mountains. There he bathed himself and painted his face with black and red paint. He fasted. He sang spirit songs. For four full days he did this. On the evening of the fourth day, it began to rain.

The rain fell for many days and many nights. Rivers swelled; lakes overflowed. Frogs and other water creatures swam around joyfully.

The people who hadn't built canoes tried to reach high ground on foot. But they discovered that all the valleys were filled with water. Trapped, these people drowned.

The people who had obeyed Beaver and built canoes began to paddle toward the mountains.

Today, of course, Mount Olympus is the tallest mountain on the Olympic Peninsula, but at that time there was one much taller. The paddlers tied their canoes to that highest mountain with the cedar ropes they had made.

Still the rain kept falling, and the world was covered, even the top of this great mountain. The people whose cedar ropes were not long enough or strong enough lost their mooring and floated away.

Once the land was covered with water, Beaver's wife said to him, "What will happen to those who come to earth after we are gone?"

For four days and nights Beaver thought about that question. Finally he decided to divide the world into two parts: the ocean, where all the waters would reside, and the land, where all the people could live. For his own use, Beaver decided to keep rivers and lakes on the land as well.

Just as the flood began to recede, the top of the tallest mountain, where all the canoes were tied, broke off. Many more canoes drifted away, and the broken top of the mountain left behind two sharp peaks connected by a long ridge. On maps today those peaks are called Mount Angeles and Blue Mountain.

The waters drew back. Land began to reappear. The people in the surviving canoes climbed out onto dry land. They followed two river valleys down out of the mountains. Today those two rivers are called the Dungeness and the Elwha. The people settled in villages near the rivers and became the ancestors of the S'Klallam people.

And the canoes that drifted away? The people in those canoes became the ancestors of other tribes that are scattered around Puget Sound and beyond.

[Adapted by Dale Faulstich from "Beaver and the Flood," told by Mrs. Jennie Talicus, interpreted by Celia Cable; and "The Flood," told by Joe Sampson, interpreted by Vera Ulmer in Klallam Folk Tales by Erna Gunther.]

THE BOY WHO DISOBEYED HIS MOTHER

When the Great Flood finally receded, the people built a village at the mouth of the Dungeness River. There a young boy lived alone with his mother. His father had provided well for the family, but one day while he was out fishing his canoe overturned and he was drowned.

Raising her son by herself, the fisherman's wife taught the boy to be a good swimmer, so that if his canoe were to overturn he would be able to save himself. Each day the boy spent hours swimming in the saltwater bay. He learned to endure the cold water and became the strongest swimmer in the village.

In the hills behind the village a small freshwater lake lay hidden by a stand of ancient cedar trees. An evil spirit lived in this lake, it was said, and the people never went there. Often, the boy's mother warned her son never to go near the haunted lake. "If you swim there," she said, "the evil spirit will grow angry and punish you."

Like most boys, the young villager didn't always listen to his mother, and like most boys he was curious. He wanted to see this lake. He crept up to it slowly, keeping behind the giant cedars. Peeking out, he saw a peaceful lake, with no sign of an evil spirit. Just looking wasn't enough, so he tossed a few small pebbles into the water. Nothing happened. He tossed a few larger stones. The lake stayed calm under the clear blue sky. No evil spirit.

Finally the boy picked up the largest rock he could and heaved it into the water. It made a great satisfying splash, and waves rolled across the surface of the lake.

Still no demon. Just a few lazy trout. The boy reached out and put his hand into the water. It was warm! Not at all like the cold salt water he was used to swimming in. The boy decided that his mother was mistaken, or that she'd made up that story about evil spirits. He took off his clothes and plunged into the lake.

All afternoon he played there. He swam and dived. He played with the small trout, trying to catch them in his hands. At last he did catch one, and as he swam to shore with it, he realized he had become very hungry. The trout would make a fine meal. He built a fire, cooked the fish, and ate. It was delicious.

As he swallowed the last bite of his little feast, the boy felt some odd twitches in his skin. Glancing down, he saw feathers growing on his arms and legs. The evil spirit had been hidden in that little trout!

He knew then that he should have obeyed his mother's warning, and he called out. But his voice didn't sound right - it was like the squawk of a loon (swákʷən). Frightened now,

Photo by Eric Dresser

he just wanted to be back home with his mother.

The boy jumped up, and to his surprise he was flying! He flew toward the village and found his mother outside on the beach. He called out again, but his mother couldn't understand him. She didn't know that the calling loon that flew around her was her son.

The sad little boy realized that no one would recognize him, and still crying he flew back to the lake. To this day, in the still morning and the early evening, you can hear the loons call out their warning: Children, always obey your mother.

[Adapted by Dale Faulstich from the story told by Elaine Grinnell in The Jamestown S'Klallam Story by Joseph H. Stauss.]

THE 18–FOOT POLE

A S'KLALLAM WARRIOR RECEIVES THE FIRST WEAPONS

Aiowasaks lived in the village at Discovery Bay. A fine warrior and the son of the chief, Aiowasaks was unfortunately also husband to a lazy, shrewish woman. One day, when their son was about twelve years old, Aiowasaks knew he could no longer live with such a mean, deceitful wife, and he did not want his son to be with her any longer either. Taking his son with him, Aiowasaks went off into the forest.

They walked for many days, eventually circling around out onto the shore of Sequim Bay. Aiowasaks decided that he needed the help of a guardian spirit. So he observed the proper rituals. He fasted. He bathed, then rubbed himself with hemlock branches. Once he was ready, he told his son to wait until he returned. Then he picked up a large stone, and holding tight to it, he jumped into Sequim Bay.

Down he went toward the very bottom of the bay, where he landed on the roof of a house. To his surprise, he heard voices coming from that drowned house.

"What has fallen on our roof?" someone asked.

Another voice replied, "That is only Aiowasaks. He has come to visit."

That house was home to the Killer Whale (qǎúmačən) People. They invited Aiowasaks in and offered him something to eat. For many days he lived with the Killer Whale People. He was always helpful and courteous to his hosts. The Killer Whale People came to respect Aiowasaks, and they felt he should be given a gift.

Asked what he wanted, he told them, "I want only to protect my family and provide for my village."

The Killer Whale People gave him a war club, a spear, a harpoon, and a bow and arrow. Then they taught him how to use these gifts and agreed to send him home.

The rear wall of the Killer Whale House had many doors. They opened one door for Aiowasaks, but it led to the S'Klallam village at Becher Bay (čiyánəxʷ) up in Canada, far from his own village. They opened another: it led to the village at the mouth of the Elwha River (ʔéʔɬxʷəʔ) still far from his home. The third door led to the village at Qatáy - Port Townsend now. This was close, but not quite close enough. They opened the fourth door, then, and told Aiowasaks to go through. He obeyed and found himself in a tunnel. He was able to walk only a short way before he fell unconscious.

His body washed up on a beach near his village on Discovery Bay. That morning the people of the village noticed a number of seagulls wheeling in to settle on something heaped on that beach. Four of the village men went in a canoe to see what was happening. They found Aiowasaks lying on the beach as if dead. Next to him lay a large number of fish; the sea gulls were feeding on these fish.

One of the village men found the war club on the beach. Another found the spear. The third man found the harpoon, and the fourth the bow and arrow.

The men gently lifted Aiowasaks into the canoe, along with the four gifts they had found on the beach. As they paddled back to the village, one of them lifted his paddle into the air every few minutes, so that the people at home would know they brought good news. When they were close enough to speak, the men shouted the news that Aiowasaks was found.

The village had missed him. They'd thought he was dead. The men carried him into his house where his wife arranged mats and blankets, doing everything she could to make him comfortable. She promised to be a better wife.

When Aiowasaks revived, he told the men where he had left his son, and they went right out to find him.

The young boy was where his father had left him, but he was completely covered in bird feathers. When he spoke, his voice was like the hoot of an owl. The boy became a powerful shaman and helped the villagers when they fell sick.

Aiowasaks used his new weapons to protect the village and provide food and wealth for his people. In this way he became a respected chief.

[Adapted by Dale Faulstich from "The Blackfish," told by David Prince in Klallam Folk Tales by Erna Gunther.]

A WOMAN MARRIES
A KILLER WHALE

It was a terrible winter, and the people were starving. The tribal hunters and gatherers could not provide for the village.

The chief's daughter and her friend went to the beach to search for shellfish. They had no luck, but they watched a Killer Whale in the bay, eating salmon. The chief's daughter said, "I wish that were my husband, so I could bring salmon for my family to eat."

Late that night, after the young woman had gone to bed, a handsome prince came to her sleeping area and spent the night with her. She awoke next morning certain that her visitor had been merely a dream. She went down to the beach again, and again she saw the Killer Whale. Again she wished the whale could be her husband. That night she had another visit from the handsome stranger.

For four days and nights the same events happened. On the fifth morning, the chief's daughter paddled a canoe out into the bay. Once she was out of sight of the village, the Killer Whale swam alongside. As she watched, the Killer Whale transformed itself into the handsome stranger. He asked her to marry him and come to his village.

38

At first the chief's daughter refused, but finally she consented. She dived out of the canoe. No sooner had she slipped under the surface of the water than she found herself in the house of her new husband. It was a large well-built longhouse, with intricately carved house posts supporting massive roof beams. Around the walls were stacked many carved and painted bentwood boxes and chests, filled with provisions of all kinds: one with salmon, one with halibut, one with other food, enough for several villages. The chief's daughter was amazed at her new husband's wealth.

On shore, at her home village, the girl's family looked for her everywhere. While they searched the beach they found many fish had floated ashore. The villagers now had plenty to eat.

A few days later, the chief's daughter came back to visit her family.

"Don't be afraid," she told them. "My new husband will catch all sorts of salmon and seafood, and I will bring it back to you."

The girl then returned to her husband, but she continued to send an abundance of fish and seafood to her home village. From time to time, the people of the village saw the princess and her husband swimming in the bay.

The village never wanted for food again, and from that time onward, whenever people from the village traveled in their canoes, they called out to the princess to calm the waters.

[Adapted by Dale Faulstich from "A Girl Marries a Sea Being," (1st version) told by Mrs. Solomon, translated by her daughter; and "A Girl Marries a Sea Being,"(2nd version) told by Mrs. Jennie Talicus, interpreted by Celia Cable, in Klallam Folk Tales by Erna Gunther.]

"Killer Whale" designed by Dale Faulstich

THE ELDERS LOUNGE POLE

WOLF AND THUNDERBIRD

Two of the most powerful guardian spirits known to the S'Klallam people, Wolf (stáʔčəŋ) and Thunderbird (čǐnəkʷaʔ) - have been carved on this pole to watch over a resource greatly valued by the Jamestown S'Klallam Tribe: the Tribal Elders.

When people in the village of Suxtcikwi'in heard wolves howl in the forest at night, they knew respect but not fear. The ancient story of the Wolf Mother (see page 16) told them that they were descendants of the wolf children, and they felt that the wolves were their friends.

It is said that the wolves never attacked anyone from this village. Instead, the wolves bestowed powerful gifts.

The S'Klallam people from Suxtcikwi'in were entitled to wear the wolf mask in dance ceremonies. One "Secret Society" ceremony that called for this wolf mask was "Xunxiani'te," a name that translates roughly as "to growl."

As a S'Klallam person's guardian spirit - one called Stat'cen - the wolf brought notable prowess as a hunter and warrior. The wolf power guaranteed bravery in the face of danger, great hunting skills, and physical agility.

There are many stories of wolves helping the S'Klallam. One tells of a village elder who was paddling his canoe up Sequim Bay one day when he saw a wolf climbing up the bank with a freshly killed seal in its jaws.

"Oh, N'esuxstonuq (my elder brother)," said the old man, "give me that seal you have so that I may feed my family. Please, let me have it."

The wolf turned its head to stare at the old grandfather. Then it dropped the seal. The wolf pushed the seal over the bank toward the elder's canoe, then stood and watched. When the man had safely loaded the seal into the canoe, the wolf wagged its tail and showed its teeth, just like a pleased dog.

Wolf is the bottom figure on this pole, shown with the elder between his paws. Above Wolf is Thunderbird. It was Wolf who introduced the power of Thunderbird to the S'Klallam people.

A gigantic and supernaturally powerful man, Thunderbird lived in the highest peaks of the Olympic Mountains. When he was hungry, Thunderbird slipped on his huge feathered cloak and at once became a great bird. His presence darkened the sky. His wings beat out thunder. Underneath those dangerous wings lived great snakes of lightning, fiery serpents Thunderbird threw down to kill whales in the ocean. Thunderbird would then seize his prey in sharp talons and carry the whale back to his mountain aerie to feast.

For the S'Klallam people, Thunderbird was one of the most feared of creatures. With some luck, however, a very brave man could earn Thunderbird as his mentor, protector, and friend. As a guardian spirit, Thunderbird blessed such a chosen man with success in hunting and fishing, and with courage in battle. These qualities earned wealth and status.

The connection between Wolf and Thunderbird is illustrated by the tale of two friends who were involved in a fierce quarrel. After much dispute, one of the two friends said, "Only the Chief of the Wolves can solve this problem. He is wise. He will tell us what is to be done."

Taking advice from the Chief of the Wolves was risky work, easier said than done. So the two friends devised a dangerous stratagem.

One of the men dragged the other over sharp barnacle-covered rocks, flaying his skin and leaving him cut and bloodied. The wounded man lay as though dying on the beach, and soon the wolves scented blood and came to claim a meal.

When the wolves carried him back to the lodge of their chief, the wounded man leaped up and declared, "I have come to seek the help and wisdom of the Chief of the Wolves!"

This man's bravery astonished the Wolves. The Chief of the Wolves rewarded his courage by teaching him the mysteries of the Thunderbird Performance. This performance became part of the "Black Tamahnous" or black-faced Sia'wen ceremonies - rituals of secret societies among high-ranking S'Klallam people.

[Adapted by Dale Faulstich from S'Klallam stories set down by Myron Eells in The Indians of Puget Sound: The Notebooks of Myron Eells, George Pierre, ed.]

TOTEM POLES AT THE 7 CEDARS CASINO

In front of the 7 Cedars Casino stands a line of seven totem poles, including a central group of three poles and two sets of paired poles.

CENTRAL GROUP, CASINO ENTRANCE, MIDDLE POLE

Of the Puget Sound Salish people, only the S'Klallam actively hunted whales and fur seal along the Pacific Coast. At the bottom of the central pole you will see the figure of a whale and a hunter. Head down as if to dive, the whale begins this pole.

Just above the whale's head, between the rising pectoral fins, a small human face represents the "blow-hole," with the dorsal fin jutting out from it. The whale hunter peers between the tail flukes, his arms and legs wrapped around the whale's body.

Above the whale and hunter is the Sun. In old Salish myth the "Chief Above," or "Old One" created the Sun to be father to all people, as the Earth is their mother. In the myth, Mother Earth is alive, the soil her flesh, the rocks her bones, the trees and the grass her hair. The wind is her breath, the water her tears.

From Earth's flesh, mixed with her tears, Old One shaped clay figures, and Sun's warmth brought them to life. These were the first, the animal people. Last of the mud-balls shaped by Old One were human beings, the most helpless of all creatures.

Shown with his beak around the Sun's corona, Raven (skʷtúʔ) is a cultural hero in many Northwest Coast Native legends, a prestigious crest figure, and an incorrigible supernatural trickster. Able to transform himself into anything at any time, Raven helped the people by putting the sun, moon, and stars into the sky, fish into the sea, salmon into the rivers, and food onto the land.

Raven, Sun, Whale and Hunter represent S'Klallam cultural history. Raven has been carved with his eyes half closed, as a symbol of the long sleep of Tribal cultural heritage during the years when S'Klallam lands and rights were obscured. Now that heritage, like Raven on this pole, experiences a new awakening.

In keeping with that idea, the paddler at the pole's top commemorates the Jamestown S'Klallam Tribe's participation in the "Paddle to Bella Bella," a contemporary canoe journey. Joined by scores of hand-carved canoes from tribes along the Northwest Coast, these challenging annual paddle journeys encourage awareness and pride in tribal heritage.

CENTRAL GROUP, LEFT-HAND POLE: T'CHITS-A-MA-HUN

An early head chief, T'Chits-a-ma-hun stood for peace between the S'Klallam and the white settlers. To him history gives credit for keeping the settlers of Port Townsend from massacre during what historians call the Indian Wars of the 1850's. (See page 14.)

On this totem pole, T'Chits-a-ma-hun holds up his hand in greeting to the early settlers. In his other hand, he holds the blanket with which he signaled the settlers of danger.

Above T'Chits-a-ma-hun is the figure of Thunderbird, a powerful guardian spirit associated with the S'Klallam people. (See page 40.)

CENTRAL GROUP, RIGHT-HAND POLE: LORD JAMES BALCH

A great leader of the S'Klallam, Lord James Balch was chief of the village near Dungeness. (See page 15.)

A people who lived almost entirely from the sea, the S'Klallam built weathertight homes from cedar along the beaches. They fished and hunted for seal and whales.

When settlers finally drove the S'Klallam from most of their lands, Lord James Balch led his people to buy land which could not be taken from them, close to a traditional village site at Dungeness. The settlement was named Jamestown in his honor.

Along with Lord James Balch on this pole are Eagle (kʷə́yŋsən) and Salmon (sčánənəxʷ), the two crest figures chosen by the Jamestown S'Klallam Tribe.

PAIRED EXTERIOR POLES AT THE 7 CEDARS CASINO

The four other poles outside the 7 Cedars Casino speak of connections. The indigenous people of the Northwest Coast made no clear separation between the natural world and the spiritual world. To succeed in the natural world, a S'Klallam person would endeavor to gain the help of one or more "spirit guardians," (as Chief Hal Ha Ske Nim, depicted on the Dance Plaza House Posts, earned the help of "The Shining One.")

The S'Klallam shared this view of the connected worlds of nature and spirit with other tribes of the Northwest. To celebrate this cultural unity, Dale Faulstich designed each of these four poles in the style of a different Northwest tribe: the Kwakwaka'wakw of the southern area; the Nuxalk of the central coast; the Haida of the Queen Charlotte Islands; and the Tlingit of the far north. (See the map on page 11.)

To complete the connection, the poles are in two pairs. The two 35-foot poles directly on either side of the central group form one pair.

The two 32-foot poles at either end of the building form another pair, each with a strong thematic link to its partner.

THE SUPERNATURAL WORLD

As you face the Casino with your back to the highway, this pole is the second from the right end of the building. Carved in the style of the Kwakwaka'wakw people of Vancouver Island, this pole represents each major realm of nature - the Forest World, the Sky World, and the Undersea World - with images of fearsome supernatural beings. Destruction followed in their wake, but to the cautious and wise they could also bring good fortune.

In the Forest lived Dzonuk'wa, the bottom figure on this pole. This "Wild Woman of the Woods" (or Basket Ogress) existed in the mythology of all the coastal peoples. The S'Klallam people know her as Slap'u (and her story is told on page 31.) Even today, our Sasquatch stories have their origin with her. Large, slow, but powerful, she brought tragedy to the unwary, though for the clever person she could be a source of great wealth.

Above Dzonuk'wa on the pole is Thunderbird. This awe-inspiring bird/ man lived high in the Olympic Mountains and was the most powerful of the supernatural spirits. Only the highest ranking and most prestigious chiefs could display Thunderbird as a crest.

The uppermost creature on this pole is Tcama'os, the Supernatural Snag. This improbable sea being assumed different forms - a floating tree stump, a giant sea lion, a whale, even a humanlike figure with a stack of potlatch cylinders rising above it (as shown on this pole). An encounter with Tcama'os could capsize a canoe; yet the cautious paddler could avoid drowning and find great prestige through the encounter.

Bold artists, the Kwakwaka'wakw modeled facial features with deep carving. Compared to the Haida style, for example, Kwakwaka'wakw faces are carved in pronounced planes that meet at well-defined angles and are set off further by generous application of varied colors. You can see that Dzonuk'wa's cheeks (painted black) rise sharply from her eye sockets (blue-green), which in turn angle abruptly in from the plane of her temples (red).

As Thunderbird's face shows, the eye is pronounced. The orb is large and rounded, almost bulging, like a truncated cone. Rather than conform to the cylinder of the log, Dzonukwa's ears and Thunderbird's beak are separate elements.

THE NATURAL WORLD

This companion to the Supernatural World is the second pole from the left end as you face the Casino. Honoring the Haida style, this pole also shows images of the Forest, Sky, and Undersea Worlds. These creatures, however, are natural beings.

At the bottom stands the Forest World's giant, Grizzly Bear, the subject of many legends (such as the story of Grizzly Bear and the Man-in-the-Moon told on page 26.) Sometimes referred to as "Elder Kinsman," the bear was treated with great respect for his strength and for his human-like qualities.

The next figure up is Raven, of the Sky World. Both hero and trickster, clown and transformer, Raven is probably portrayed more often than any other creature in Northwest Coast art. The mythology of the entire region is feathered with Raven's exploits.

At top, from the Undersea World, is Killer Whale, also called Blackfish. A figure of awe, as the stories on the South Campus Poles reveal, Killer Whale interacted with the seafaring coastal people in daily life as well as in legend.

The Natural World pole shows restraint in the use of color, with black, red, and blue-green added only to accent the carving. The stretches of undecorated wood highlight other features of the Haida style.

On Grizzly Bear's face, for example, the forehead slopes back slightly from the broad semi-angular eyebrows. Grizzly's eye sockets are clearly defined by their hollow ovoid shape as well as by the blue-green paint. The eye itself is more deeply carved underneath. The line of Grizzly's eyelid has been both carved and painted for emphasis. The eye is slightly constricted at each end, and the iris is large, round, and solid black.

Grizzly's nose, like Raven's beak, is bent down sharply to conform to the basic cylinder shape of the log, the nostrils of each figure large with a moderate flair.

The two poles at each end of the Casino are the final pairing. Although most of the Jamestown poles depict people, animals, and supernatural creatures, the carved figures in Northwest Coast Art can also represent natural phenomena such as clouds, rainbows, celestial bodies - and even abstract ideas - in three dimensions. These elements usually appear in human form.

On these companion poles, the subjects are Elements from Nature and, appropriate to the Casino, the Elements for Success.

ELEMENTS FROM NATURE

The humanlike forms of this pole at the far right end of the 7 Cedars Casino building represent natural phenomena. As a seafaring culture, for example, the people of the Northwest Coast had great respect for - and a healthy fear of - Fog Woman. The bottom figure on the pole, she was a frequent visitor to the coastal areas. As an ally, she concealed a person from enemies, or allowed a hunter extra stealth in approaching the prey.

Woe to the person who earned her enmity, however. He would become disoriented and might never find the way home again.

The showy figure above Fog Woman is a personification of Rainbow, also called "Supernatural-One-Upon-Whom-It-Thunders." Chief of all the supernatural beings of the forest, Rainbow would choose his time to appear. Then, dressed in gorgeous regalia, a cloak of many colors, he danced across the sky.

The next figure on this pole is Cloud Woman. Most totem carvers portray her as a human with birdlike features. Here she has a beak and feathered limbs. Cloud Woman was, naturally, a person of very high status, and her home was in the sea. When Cloud Woman felt the time was right, she left her sea home to fly up into the sky.

Cumulus Clouds, the three small figures at the very top, accompany Cloud Woman on this pole. Their tapered caps represent wisps of cloud.

The Tlingit style, reflected in these carvings, typically features rounded contours on the face. You can see this characteristic roundness in Fog Woman's curved eyebrows and noticeable eyelid over a pronounced, deep-set eye. Notice that each figure's iris is large and round, the whites barely constricted at either end. The flared nostrils on Fog Woman's nose are typical of Tlingit style, and even Rainbow and Cloud Woman have flared nostrils beneath their beaky noses. The figures have slightly open mouths, with well-developed lips and visible teeth.

ELEMENTS FOR SUCCESS

If its companion shows elements of nature, this pole at the far left end of the Casino represents elements as far removed from the natural world as we care to go. Illustrated on this pole are the elements necessary to operate a successful Casino.

The bottom figure is the most crucial element. The Eagle (kʷə́yŋsən) holding a Salmon (sčánənəxʷ) in its talons represents the Jamestown S'Klallam Tribe. The vision and guidance of the Tribal Council, and the consent of the Tribe's citizens, form the basis for success in all of the Tribe's business ventures.

Any successful venture needs financial backing, too, so the next figure portrayed on the pole is the Financier. Carved as a prosperous chief, he holds a fine copper shield and wears a potlatch hat, both symbols of wealth and status. The hawk-like features of the Financier's face, however, warn us to be careful; he is a bird of prey.

Precariously grasping the Financier's hat and hoping to acquire some of his wealth is the next important figure - the Gambler.

At the top is the final ingredient for success, the necessary evil of government oversight. This last element is portrayed as a mouse, the little rodent that eats at every man's table.

The Nuxalk style reflected in this pole is noted for strong intersecting planes of convex and concave surfaces. Brows are usually heavy and eye sockets deep-set and well-defined, as you can see on the Eagle.

The eye socket flows into a distinctive cheek bulge at the outer corner of the orb. The Financier's face shows how in Nuxalk carving the orb of the eye is a truncated cone, and the eye itself is round and flat.

The nostrils are clearly defined and flaring, and the lips often left slightly parted. Added elements such as Eagle's beak or Financier's nose have an upward thrust.

Despite the strength of the features in the Nuxalk style, the colors (black, red, blue-green, and another strong blue) do not necessarily follow the carved planes of the face. Notice how the bright "Bella Coola blue" in the Financier's face follows its own painted geometry, regardless of the underlying shapes of cheek and eye.

CONCLUSION

The paired poles at the 7 Cedars Casino represent the range and energy of Northwest Coast Art. The whole collection of poles reflects the vitality of the Jamestown S'Klallam Tribe itself.

The stories of the Founding Fathers, carved on the Dance Plaza House Posts, oversee the administrative offices of a Tribal leadership that has achieved national prominence in issues of tribal self-governance.

Like the poles outside the 7 Cedars Casino, some future totem poles will stand outside the Longhouse Market and Deli complex; a planned resort hotel and Conference Center; a new Family Health and Medical Center; and the Cedars at Dungeness Golf Course and Restaurant. These are the newest of many business ventures of a Tribe focused on accountability, independence and contribution to the local economy.

Stories on the Legends and South Campus poles emphasize community and a deep bond with nature. Both those crucial strengths are reflected in the Jamestown S'Klallam Tribe's outreach in such areas as health care - with a new medical and dental complex - and ecology - with natural resources research, watershed rehabilitation, and habitat restoration. The programs benefit not only Jamestown Tribal citizens but also everyone who lives and works on the Olympic Peninsula.

The totem poles now standing on the Jamestown S'Klallam Tribal property, and those to come, will continue to honor the past, present, and future of "the Strong People."

Dale Faulstich and Nathan Gilles applying the finishing touches to the Longhouse Market totem poles.

BIBLIOGRAPHY

Barbeau, Marius. <u>Totem Poles: According to Crests and Topics</u>. Vol.I. Quebec: Canadian Museum of Civilization, 1990.

Barbeau, Marius. <u>Totem Poles: According to Location</u>. Vol.II. Quebec: Canadian Museum of Civilization, 1990.

Clark, Ella. <u>Indian Legends of the Pacific Northwest</u>. Berkeley, California: University of California Press, 1953.

Eells, Myron. <u>The Indians of Puget Sound: The Notebooks of Myron Eells</u>. Edited and Introduction by George Pierre Castile. Seattle: University of Washington Press, 1985.

Elmendorf, William W. <u>Twana Narratives: Native Historical Accounts of a Coast Salish Culture</u>. Seattle: University of Washington Press, 1993.

Gorsline, Jerry, Ed. <u>Shadows of Our Ancestors: Readings in the History of Klallam-White Relations</u>. Dalmo'ma Anthology Vol. Viii. Port Townsend, Washington: Empty Bowl Press, 1992.

Gunther, Erna. <u>Ethnobotany of Western Washington</u>. University of Washington Publications in Anthropology. Vol.X, No.1. Seattle: University of Washington Press, 1973.

Gunther, Erna. <u>Klallam Ethnography</u>. University of Washington Publications in Anthropology. Vol.1, No.5, pp.171-314. Seattle: University of Washington Press, 1927.

Gunther, Erna. <u>Klallam Folk Tales</u>. University of Washington Publications in Anthropology. Vol.1, No.4, pp 113-170. Seattle: University of Washington Press, 1925.

Hilbert, Vi. <u>Haboo: Native American Stories from Puget Sound</u>. Seattle: University of Washington Press, 1988.

Holm, Bill. "Form in NorthWest Art." Chapter 2 in Roy L. Carlson, <u>Indian Art Traditions of the Northwest Coast</u>. Simon Fraser University, Burnaby B.C.:Archaeology Press,1976.

Jamestown S'Klallam Tribe. <u>Special Blessing of the Dance Plaza House Posts: December 4, 2004</u>. Compact Disk. Port Townsend, Washington: Long Light Productions, 2005.

Lambert, Mary Ann. <u>The House of the Seven Brothers + Trees,Roots, and Branches of the House of Ste-Tee-Thlum + A Genealogical Story of the Olympic Peninsula Clallam Indians</u>. np:nd. Inscribed "Mary Ann Lambert Vincent, Oct. 27, 1960."

Macdonald, George F. <u>Haida Monumental Art: Villages of the Queen Charlotte Islands</u>. Vancouver, B.C.: University of British Columbia Press, 1994.

Smyly, John and Carolyn. <u>Those Born at Koona: The Totem Poles of the Haida Village Skedans, Queen Charlotte Island</u>. Surrey, B.C.: Hancock House Publishers, 1994.

Stauss, Joseph. H. <u>The Jamestown S'Klallam Story: Rebuilding a Northwest Coast Indian Tribe</u>. Sequim, Washington: Jamestown S'Klallam Tribe, 2002.

Stewart, Hilary. <u>Cedar</u>. Seattle: University of Washington Press, 1984.

Stewart, Hilary. <u>Looking at Totem Poles</u>. Seattle: University of Washington Press, 1993.

Suttles, Wayne. <u>Coast Salish Essays</u>. Seattle: University of Washington Press, 1987.

Wright, Robin K. <u>A Time of Gathering: Native Heritage in Washington State</u>. Catalogue for Washington State Centennial Exhibit, 1989. Burke Museum, Seattle: University of Washington Press, 1991.

BIOGRAPHIES

Dale Faulstich, Designer and Lead Carver for the Jamestown Totem Poles, has lived and worked on the Northwest coast since 1972. In addition to ongoing projects and classes for the Tribe, Dale continues his own contemporary applications of Northwest style. He has created masks, steam bent boxes, animal form bowls, rattles, drums, and ceremonial objects, as well as carved doors, wall panels, furniture, fine art prints, sculpture and other contemporary applications which can be found in many private and corporate collections across the U.S. His work is shown at Northwest Native Expressions Gallery in Sequim, Washington; Stonington Gallery at Pioneer Square in Seattle; and Pacific Traditions Gallery in Port Townsend.

Joan Worley is a freelance writer living in Sequim, Washington. A former teacher, she holds a Ph.D. in Comparative Literature from Ohio University.

David Woodcock is an award-winning professional aerial photographer living in Sequim. Also specializing in landscape and wildlife photography, David has photographed extensively around the Pacific Northwest as well as Canada and Alaska. He was an honor graduate of the University of Washington School of Dentistry in 1971 and works as a contract dentist with the Jamestown S'Klallam Tribe. Contact David at www.greywolfphotography.com